WEC Centennial Children's Book

The Golden Chariot

True stories of God at work

WEC Centennial Children's Book

The Golden Chariot
True stories of God at work

By kids from around
the world

CF4·K

10 9 8 7 6 5 4 3 2 1
© Copyright 2012 WEC International
ISBN: 978-1-84550-981-1

Published by
Christian Focus Publications,
Geanies House, Fearn, Ross-shire,
IV20 1TW, Scotland, UK.
www.christianfocus.com
e-mail: info@christianfocus.com

Cover design by Daniel van Straaten
Illustrated by Miguel Borham
Printed and bound by Bell and Bain, Glasgow

MIX
Paper from
responsible sources
FSC® C007785

Contents

God's Love

Introduction

When parents are called by God to work in foreign countries people often ask, 'So what about the kids?' These stories, written by the kids themselves, will give you an insight into their lives.

As we celebrate 100 years of WEC, we want to share stories from kids whose parents have worked in different parts of the world. Some of the families still live abroad, while others have already returned to their home countries.

These kids have found that God includes **them** in what He is doing. Some were present during major events in world history, while others have risked their lives on fast-flowing, crocodile-infested rivers. We refer to them as Third Culture Kids (TCKs): kids who have spent a significant part of their lives in more than one culture, and taken on aspects of each culture.

Our WEC kids grow up knowing how much their Father cares for them, in big areas as well as small. Some have struggled to discover where they fit in, while others have escaped from guerillas in war-torn countries. Some have been stranded in the jungle, and others have just needed friends.

One teacher in a home country said, 'I always know when there's a TCK in the class – they have such a depth of experience and understanding, greater than most other kids of their age.'

These are exciting, true stories, written by modern-day kids whose parents are part of a company that is now 100 years old. Our young writers reflect our multinational company; they come from Australia, Australia/Peru, Brazil, Brazil/South Africa, Germany, Korea, The Netherlands, New Zealand, Nigeria, United Kingdom, United States.

It has been a delight to work with these stories. I hope you enjoy them as much as I do!

My special thanks to my two main assistants in this project, Angie Ross-Watson and Michelle Kallmier. And huge thanks to that amazing, talented group of MKs who wrote the stories!

The person to whom we are all indebted for the wonderful illustrations is an MK from Spain/Australia, Miguel Borham. Thanks for the many hours you put into this, Miguel.

Jen Kallmier

Footnote: You can learn more about the countries mentioned in this book from the world prayer guide *Operation World* by Jason Mandryk, or on the *Operation World* website: www.operationworld.org

Escape Stories

About two hours from our small town, we had a toilet break, and I forgot, like a silly person, to put my seat belt back on! Soon came the highest mountain pass on the route, which on this day was sunny on one side and had snowed on the other. You can see where this is going...

As my dad was coming out of the sunny side, the road became very slightly icy. We skidded. Dad said, 'Oh no, we're going, WE'RE GOING!!!' and he was right, we really did go. After that it was a blur.

There were some tiny little red-and-white posts in the way. We smashed through them like a cannon against wood at point-blank range. Then there was a steep slope straight down the mountain side. We rolled twice like a washing machine. The boot door was ripped off and all our stuff rolled away.

It was very frightening, but miraculously we landed back on our wheels a long way from the road. Although we were really shaken up, we were alive! The whole family loudly praised God again.

Some windows had imploded, leaving Dad with a nasty cut. Our car was battered and crushed all over. My little brother's second-hand chair had kept him safe (we'd always thought it was a piece of junk but it worked!).

As for me, this is a bit of a mystery, but it felt as if I had a seat belt on! There was tons of stuff flying about from the boot, but none of it hit anyone in the car. I had a bump on my head, my back hurt a bit, and I couldn't breathe very well for a few moments, but apart from that I was unhurt.

It was freezing on the mountainside, but while we were gathering up our stuff, I said weakly, 'The Golden Chariot protected us.' It was amazing.

Some friendly truck drivers took Mum, me and my brother home. Dad managed to stuff all our things in the car and put some ropes over the boot. There was a small dirt track that came onto the road about a mile away cross country, and Dad went along that, even crossing a river to get there. Then he drove back to the city through blizzards, winds and rain. He said it was, 'bloomin' cold'!

We have been back there since, on our way to our small town home. We've even gathered up some more stuff we missed the first time, like some of Mum's make-up!

God has given me an experience I will never forget, and I am very grateful. From then on my prayer before a long drive has been: 'God please send the golden chariot to protect us.'

Seth – aged 10

The Bible says that God has ordered his angels to protect us wherever we go.[1] Seth and his family always thank God for his protection when they travel! They have lived in China for six years. Seth enjoys designing buildings and hopes to run a falconry centre one day.

---

[1] Psalm 91:11

What a Team!

Dad and I were working on our bush airstrip in Kalimantan. It was getting dark and it was time to go home. We hurried down to our longboat moored at the lake. Its edge now lapped the airstrip and joined with the flooded black waters of the Ketungau River nearly a kilometre away.

As my dad pulled the starter on our eighteen horsepower outboard, it stalled, and the bow wave came over the back of the boat. We sank, and were left treading water with just the tip of the boat's bow visible. The fuel tank bobbed peacefully on the water. If it wasn't for my dad being a poor swimmer and both of us having our boots on, it would have been funny. The tropical darkness was now nearly complete and my dad started to panic as he tried to swim in his boots. As a boy Dad had nearly drowned and was never a confident or capable swimmer.

For the first time in my young life, I had to take the lead. I was eight years old. It was a life or death situation. My dad could drown! I was a much better swimmer, so I was able to tread water while taking off my boots. If you think it's easy, try it sometime! My dad couldn't do it. 'Dad,' I yelled, 'grab on to a tree'. There were quite a few small trees sticking out of the flooded lake near where we sank. Dad was able to hold on to a tree while taking off his boots.

We swam from one tree to another, stopping often for my dad to catch his breath, until we reached the airstrip. Then we walked across the airstrip, just about the only piece of dry, cleared land for miles around. From there we began to cross the flooded riverine rainforest, full of spiky vines and bamboo, poisonous snakes, biting insects, aggressive fish and even crocodiles – and all in the dark!

It was pitch black. Now it was Dad's turn to help me. The water was deep, dark and cold, over my head and up to Dad's chest. Strips of thorny rattan branches reached out to cruelly cut into us as we waded through the water. Splash! Something cold and slimy brushed my leg!

After what seemed like ages we could see more light. It must be the riverbank. Then suddenly the sound of a motorboat chugging slowly upriver. Dad called out, but was unheard over the boat engine. It was my turn to take the lead again. I swam out to a tree at the main river's edge and climbed up, waving my arms. The boat was slowing down. We were safe!

Soon we had warm towels and hot tea from the Malay boat crew. They became our firm friends, never forgetting the rescue of the white man and his boy. I believe God protected us in so many ways that night and used the skills that each of us had for his glory. What a team!

Paul Rattray

Paul's Dayak friends in Kalimantan taught him how to swim – and how to eat jungle food, including snails! Paul now lives in Australia with his wife and children. He regularly travels in South East Asia as a project manager in media and missions work, reaching unreached peoples with the gospel. Paul occasionally returns to Kalimantan.

I was going to die. We were all panicking. The first thing my dad said to us was to pray, which we did.

We needed to find some way to get out of the car. There was only one place that was not blocked by branches, so my dad wound down the side window and we all climbed out.

A 'chowkidar' (the guard outside a house) saw what had happened. He gestured to us to come and shelter in the house. We ran through the rain. Then we heard a loud thump and saw another tree falling down. It fell exactly where we had run to get to this house.

We were amazed at the kindness of the people in the house. They gave us tea and biscuits. Soon the 'chowkidar' helped us find a taxi, which managed to get us home.

The policemen who eventually came and saw the scene were amazed that we had survived.

When we arrived home it was still raining hard and the electricity was off. We sat round our dining table and talked about what had happened. I just couldn't help crying. Different thoughts came to us like, 'how had the car been so badly damaged, but none of us were hurt?' and 'it's amazing how God saved us'.

A couple of days later my dad said to us all, 'you know, we had prayed for a new car, and God has remarkably used these circumstances to give us a new one.'

This story really shows God's power. An enormous tree fell on us but He kept us safe.

Faith – aged 12

The Bible says, 'I will not leave you, I will never abandon you'.[1]

God has so often protected His children as they serve Him in difficult places. Faith and her family experienced this a number of times, as they lived in Pakistan for many years.

---

[1] Hebrews 13:5

Dangerous Escape

Even though I was very young, the following events could have changed my life dramatically and when I think about the story now that I'm older, it's scary to think about what could have happened.

The events took place in what is now called the Democratic Republic of Congo. The year was 1997. At the time we were living in the heart of the dense Zairean rainforest that covers most of the country.

Why were we there? Congo once belonged to Belgium. The Belgians had built roads and several hospitals in the forest, but ever since Congo had been given independence from Belgium, nearly everything had been reclaimed by the forest. My dad was involved in a boat building project. It involved teaching the locals how to build boats so that they could travel and trade on the river. My mum was home-schooling my sisters, and I was only a baby who did nothing but gurgle at everything.

Life in the forest was very basic; we had limited supplies of processed food and basic everyday items. We lived off the forest and cooked on a basic wood stove. The scariest thing was the solitude; we had no communication with the outside world, except through satellite phones.

During this time a number of African countries were going into civil war following the Rwanda genocide. While we were in the Congo, civil war broke out, but this wasn't a major problem for us because we were in the middle of nowhere. The problem for us was the rebels from Rwanda who had escaped their corrupt country. They were heading for our village and, being poor and hungry, they may have been hoping to get their hands on any equipment or items of value.

We heard word of this, so my dad radioed for MAF to land at the airstrip that had just been finished. MAF needed to make sure that their plane would not be shot down or stolen when they landed! MAF agreed to send a plane if we would leave a signal – a white sheet laid out on the airstrip. Somehow someone managed to get hold of a plain white sheet. Soon the aircraft landed and we managed to get out of the forest just in time. We were among the last expatriate families to be evacuated from the country. All the local people fled into the forest to avoid the soldiers.

Half an hour later, our village was looted and our house was stripped down to hardly anything. Even the glass was taken from the windows, along with anything else that could be used or sold.

We still weren't safe. We had flown into a thunderstorm and there was extreme turbulence that made the plane feel like a paper plane. Somehow we got through the storm, with the plane and everybody in it intact. We were headed for Central African Republic. Suddenly there was the sound of bombs going off, and there were shells exploding in the air around the plane. My dad was wearing the spare set

of headphones and he was horrified to hear that the country we were travelling into had just declared civil war.

We finally landed at an airport, where our passports were taken from us. Now we were refugees! News got through to our grandparents and friends, and everybody back home was praying for our family. It was a tense time. After a few days the passports were returned and we headed for the UK. What a relief!

Joseph Beakhouse – aged 15

Psalm 27:5 says, 'In the day of trouble he will keep me safe.' Joseph, with his mum and dad and two older sisters, were many times aware of God's protection. Joseph has always had an interest in planes. He would like to become an aerospace engineer in the future, and work with MAF anywhere in the world.

Miracle Boy

My name is Danny and I am a miracle boy. Why? Well, you'll see ...

When I was one year old, I drank bleach. When I was two, I lost my family at a big airport in Asia. Then when I was six I was hit by a car.

But the story I am going to tell you right now is the one of the best miracle stories. I was two years old. We lived in a tall apartment building which was seven storeys tall. Our apartment was on the fifth floor. That day Mum's friend came over to talk. My sister was playing in the living room by my mum.

Meanwhile, I was in my room playing. I climbed onto my tricycle, rode onto the windowsill and out the window! I was hanging onto the other side of the windowsill. I called my mum three times because I was stuck.

Mum thought it was weird because I usually came to her and called her. So she came into my room, but I wasn't there. She looked out the window and saw where I was hanging off the sill. Mum grabbed me and brought me back into the house!

After that event my mum could not close her eyes. Every time she did she would see me falling down to the bottom of our building. Finally, my dad put his hand on her and prayed. Mum saw a vision that many angels were surrounding me while I was out there hanging from the window sill.

That is the end of the story. Why am I called a miracle boy? Because my mum saw a vision that I was protected by angels when I was outside the window.

Danny Kang – aged 8

Danny's parents have had to trust God to work overtime keeping an eye on him! Check out Matthew 18:10, 11 in the Bible. What does it say about children and angels? Danny and his family live in a big country in Asia. He wants to be a vet who travels around the world. Danny loves animals and wants to help them.

The Riot

It was a Thursday afternoon and we were on the way to Dakar, Senegal's capital city. My parents and I had just picked up Thomas, my older brother, from Bourofaye Christian School (BCS) for the midterm break. After six weeks apart, we were really looking forward to our time together.

In one of the towns on the way there is a huge cement factory. As we approached the town we saw a long traffic jam building up in front of us. We wanted to get to Dakar as quickly as possible and not get stuck in a traffic jam for hours. Some cars in front of us left the road and took a narrow dirt track over railway lines and into a housing estate. We followed them.

As we approached the single-storey cement houses with their corrugated roofs, a group of very angry young men appeared from nowhere and blocked the 'road'. Within seconds there were about 100 young people, some armed with iron bars. Our car was surrounded.

The men were screaming at us in French and tapping the windows with the iron bars. Neither my mum nor dad spoke French, and we didn't know what was happening. My mum tried to talk to the young

War in Africa

In 2002 the civil war in Cote d'Ivoire began. The war was exciting and scary for my friends and I. It was also strange, since we didn't understand why so many had to die for power that seemed worthless to us and could be easily taken away.

My parents were working in the WEC guest house in Abidjan, while I lived with my sister, Philippa (13) and brother, Zac (8) in a boarding school outside a little village called Vavoua.

One night, my dorm mother told me that the rebels were in Abidjan, and my mum and dad were stuck in the guesthouse. They couldn't go in or out because there was fighting right outside. They could hear and see the shots.

Horrible pictures raced through my mind ... What if the rebels got into the guesthouse and started shooting? What if the fighting never stopped and I couldn't get to my mum and dad? What if mum or dad got kidnapped, or shot? What if Philippa, Zac and I became orphans – how would we get home?

I went into my room and hugged my big pink teddy that I had named 'Mother', and began to cry.

At lunch the next day Philippa ran up and yelled, 'Rhyanna, guess what!! The fighting has stopped and Mum and Dad can get out again!' I was SO happy. Philippa and I jumped around in circles. Zac wanted to know what was going on, but we decided not to tell him since he was too young.

Apart from regular updates on the war, life went on as normal. A few people came from nearby villages to take refuge at our school, which was fun because they brought more kids who we could play with. Then one Tuesday we were told to pack up, as we were going to evacuate on Friday.

The next afternoon the fire alarm went off. Uncle André called for silence. 'This is not a fire drill. The rebels are in Seguela, which is a forty-five minute drive away; they could be heading here right now. We need to leave now.'

At that point everyone was really scared, but Uncle André quietened us down and prayed. Then he told us, 'Go to your classrooms and get what you need, then go to your dorms, pack one suitcase between a family, and if you are an only child then share with at least one other person.'

I grabbed the biggest trunk I had and we packed everything that Philippa, Zac and I needed. My dorm mother told me I shouldn't bring my toys since they were big and would take too much room. I was really upset and kept wondering how I could smuggle them into one of the cars.

The big blue truck stopped outside my dorm and I practically leapt for joy. I could easily smuggle my toys on board. I shoved them underneath the seats.

At last we all bundled into cars to set out on what we thought of as a great adventure. We would go to Abidjan, wait for it to all settle down, and then come back. It was really nice when one of the workers from the village ran around handing out chocolate ice creams!!

As we drove on, it got dark. I was about to go to sleep when Aunty Heather told the driver to stop, as the two cars behind us had stopped. We were all ready to tumble out, but she told us firmly to stay in the car. I could see the adults walking back and forth between the cars, or huddling in groups and whispering.

I could tell that my little brother was scared. It was dark and we were in the middle of a road, with forest stretched out as far as we could see on both sides of the road. I was scared but I was trying not to show it since I was the oldest in the car. One boy told me that he was scared because he was imagining the rebels coming out of the forest and starting to shoot or take everyone hostage.

We talked about escape routes and what we would do if we ran into the forest and had to survive in the jungle. I said not to worry, and to imagine the rebels turning into silly clowns and their guns turning to water pistols and their cars turning into those really small cars that clowns all cram into and drive around in. This made him feel a bit better, but it didn't really help me.

Finally, the door opened and two more people crammed in. The last car had run over a pothole and both tyres on the left side were shredded. It was too hard to fix the tyres in the dark. They decided to leave the car there and cram everyone in different cars and go to Bouafle to stay with friends.

We stopped again at a roadblock. There was a 6.00 pm curfew and anyone on the streets after six would be shot.

We went to a church by the side of the road. The pastor gladly invited us to stay. We had tea and then arranged where to sleep. There were three mattresses, and my teddies were brought out as pillows and cushions. The church pews were beams of wood, with uncomfortable gaps between them.

I barely slept at all. But I do remember having a dream of everyone gathered in a circle praying, and that we were safe and out of harm's way. After that dream I was a lot calmer and I believe it was God's way of reassuring me that we would all make it safely to Abidjan.

The next day some guys went off in the big blue truck while we sang praises to God and told riddles and jokes and played other games. After some hours they came back with the fixed car and everyone gave a huge cheer!! We went on to Bouafle and met the WEC leaders there. They gave us ice creams and we kids played hide and seek and tag, climbed trees and got into trouble for picking the flowers. It was heaps of fun!

We were supposed to go on to Abidjan but had to stay another few days in Bouafle since there was a massive protest in Abidjan. There were pictures of it on the T.V. and the streets were packed with people.

I was happy when we finally left as I really wanted to see my mum and dad. We all arrived safely at the guesthouse and I gave my parents a gigantic hug! Then I drilled them with all the questions I had saved up for them.

Rhyanna George – written when she was 15 years old

Rhyanna was 11 years old when the rebellion started. She is now studying veterinary science in South Australia. Rhyanna hopes to work as a vet in West Africa. The experience of living among the poor and seeing a country in civil war has given her a keener perspective on what's important in life.

God's Protection

Creepy-Crawlies

I am frightened of creepy-crawlies. Where we lived, in Northern Cambodia, there were all sorts of creepy crawlies. Lots of times I found insects in the bathroom. It wasn't even an outside bathroom, mind you. It was inside. I didn't dare to go in there for quite some time!

There were all sorts of bugs. There were huge rhinoceros beetles that could cling to you with their sharp pincers. There were little insects that flew around after rain, and dropped their wings everywhere. There were also huge grasshoppers, and praying mantises.

One day, I was walking through the house, and trod on a scorpion. Now, I have no idea how it got in. There were some very steep steps in our house, and the house had been closed up for a few days. I had seen the scorpion before, but I had thought it was a squashed bug. Very silly of me! I had forgotten all about it, until I trod on it.

It felt a bit like a sudden bad burn. It hurt badly. A scorpion sting is very dangerous, especially for a child. Mum had a thing that sucks out stings. We used that, only we couldn't immediately identify the place where I had been stung.

Dad stomped on the scorpion with his shoe. It came to a sudden and sticky sudden end.

Mum rang up a team member who was a doctor. She said to elevate the leg. Mum prayed for me. She slept in the bed with me, in case I had a reaction in the night. What if I had difficulty breathing in the middle of the night? There was no proper medical help in the whole province. Most people have a lot of pain for days after a scorpion sting.

Nothing happened.

I woke up in the morning needing the toilet. The foot just felt a bit tingly. To be honest, it didn't hurt at all. Dad told me that I would have to wear shoes all the time from now on. I don't mind!

Mum told me that this would be a good story to tell my friends when I was a teenager. I'm glad it has a happy ending, and that Jesus kept me safe from the scorpion's sting!

Kimberley Saunders, aged 9

Everyone loved ... ... with his parents and ... ... reading, and outside she loves ... but NOT bugs or scorpions!

Journey of Faith

'And Abraham went, even though he did not know where he was going ...' [1]

Have you ever wondered how Abraham felt, following and believing God only by trust, and faith that God would guide him through his journey? He had no idea what he would find, or where God was leading him; all he did was obey ...

In my case, it wasn't that we (my family) did not know where we were going, but we began our journey trusting God to help us reach our destination.

My parents are Christian workers in the Gambia, and I was born there. As a family, we rarely visited our home country, Nigeria, and finally in 2008, my dad decided that we had to go there for Christmas. His parents were getting old, and we had not seen them as an entire family for six years. They had never seen my four-year-old brother.

My mum was strongly against it because we could not afford to fly, but seeing that my dad was determined, she gave in, deciding to have faith as my dad suggested. My parents then agreed that since we could not go by plane we should go by car.

---

[1] Hebrews 11:8

The journey was exciting and fun for the first few days. We passed through Senegal without many problems.

When we drove through Mali it was night. A policeman warned us of certain areas that were extremely dangerous and where we should be careful.

As we were passing through one of those areas we saw a sign that said 'danger' – our second warning. My dad drove through anyway because we had no choice – it was night and we were in a foreign country.

We were alright for the first few kilometers when suddenly our car spluttered, and with an enormous groan the engine died.

The road was deserted, and even if there were passers-by we would have found it difficult to ask for help in a place marked dangerous. The night was pitch black and the road was lonely. We were foreigners in Mali – a perfect target for armed robbers. There weren't houses or hotels for us to stop at, or lights to guide the way.

My mum woke me and my siblings and together we prayed while my dad tried to find the solution to our dilemma.

After fruitless attempts to fix our car my dad had an idea ... to tie the damaged parts of our car together ... and it worked! Our car engine came alive once more and carried us to a safer environment.

We thanked God for giving my dad that idea!

During the rest of our journey to Nigeria (which took a week) we, as a family, saw God work in many more ways. It was an awesome experience, though frightening and exhausting too, and God taught us a lot about trusting him and going by faith ... I am so glad that we did it!

Deborah Meribole – aged 15

Deborah has lived in The Gambia all her life, although she attends an MK school in Senegal. Travel in Africa can sometimes be dangerous. If you know someone who lives in Africa, would you like to pray for them?

After a bit of a walk we came to a little shed in the trees. There were loads of puppies just in front of us running towards the trees and hiding. We watched until all of them disappeared into the trees, then we walked around the shed to see more. Suddenly there were about 12-15 dogs – scruffy, thin, hungry-looking dogs – all staring at us and kind of prowling.

It was scary. We were surrounded by bushes. We were afraid to run for it in case they ran after us. In this country many stray dogs are rabid. Often they have stones thrown at them so they become unpredictable and sometimes bite. Even if we saw one stray dog it could be scary, but seeing this many together was freaky.

Mum grabbed my hand and started praying quietly while I was looking at the dogs. The closest one was three metres from us.

I huddled into Mum, but then I noticed something – the dogs were now looking at us casually and then looking away, not bothering about us.

After what seemed like a long time, we got out of there only by Jesus' protecting hand on us. When we got back to the hotel the others were waiting for us and Dad gave us an 'Are you okay?' glance, probably because Mum and I were so pale after what happened.

After a bit we told them what happened and headed home. That night I was thanking God for keeping us safe from those dogs.

Alasdair – aged 13

Animals that are not cared for sometimes become aggressive. This is one of the many dangers Alasdair and his family have to watch out for in this Central Asian country where they have lived for ten years. Alasdair would like to be an engineer one day.

the faces of those who had been fighting it. It cooled them off as well as the burnt bush.

We went back to our supper only to find it covered with fine soot that had filtered through the screens. Hungry, we ate it anyway.

That night the air was so sharp and acrid it hurt our noses to breathe. I tried not to complain. After all, God had put out the fire and we were thankful for that, even if a little uncomfortable with the leftovers.

Marilyn Mertz (teacher),
Vavoua International School, Cote d'Ivoire (1979-1999)

Teachers at schools for TCKs[1] need to be flexible – unexpected things often happen! They have such an important influence on the kids. Pray for more teachers, with a love for God and for kids, to be willing to teach in foreign countries.

---

[1] Third Culture Kids (see Introduction)

Rat Attack

It was midnight Friday, going on Saturday, and we were on senior weekend ... Friday had been great – squishing into a real bus (with 'real' brakes) and then heading off to spend the weekend relaxing, messing around and – best of all – escape from the juniors! Green swimming pool, mouldy mango trees and all, the first day at the hotel was great! I was looking forward to the following day, but first ... I had to survive the night.

I collapsed on a lumpy mattress on the floor surrounded by nine other guys all trying to get to sleep and the thing I remember most of all was the stifling heat. The AC was broken and the room smelled strongly of male body odour and chlorine.

We tossed and turned until somebody, I think it was Michel, had a brainwave and decided to open our door to get some cool wind coming through. This had no effect whatsoever on the boiling temperature of the room, and we were immediately invaded by legions of bloodthirsty mosquitoes! After buying a mosquito coil and emptying several bottles of repellent into the room, one by one we dropped off to sleep ...

That was when a large, furred creature must have scurried through our open door. Michel, who had dumped his mattress in front of the entrance, did not even stir at this intrusion despite the puddle of still damp pee that we discovered on his mattress the next morning. (There have been debates as to whether or not the rat was responsible.)

The first one to be disturbed was Tristan, who felt something scratching his back and, believing it was a kitten, smacked it away, then whiskers brushed against his face and he opened his eyes to see an elephantine rat bouncing away across the room!

I remember hearing yells of 'RAT!!' and then several piercing screams that would have put a girl to shame. Half-awake, I sat up only to see a huge black rat dash across my legs leaving a scratch mark along one ankle. I will admit I leapt up onto the bed near me, joining the three other guys already there!

The rat ran back towards the freedom of the outside garden, leaving a trail of guys standing on anything the rat couldn't get to, but was thwarted when Uncle Simon hurled something at it from a safe distance, forcing it to change direction and disappear into the bathroom! Four guys immediately slammed the door shut and locked it tight!

Sometime later, about three in the morning (none of us could sleep with the rat still in the bathroom), Max left quietly only to return with three massive poles. He gave one to Ismael and they slowly unlocked the bathroom door, followed by a film crew of cautious guys holding cameras! The rat couldn't be seen anywhere … only an overturned bin in the shower remained a mystery.

Max crept towards it, brandishing his enormous sticks, and peered over the edge of the bin. Max gave the thumbs up and slowly aimed at a football with his stick, as if he were playing golf. He thwacked the ball with an almighty thud and it flew into the bin! An agonised squeak came from inside and Max edged closer. Suddenly a long tail appeared from behind the ball and it was soon followed by a desperate rat! The rat streaked across the tiled floor, but it was not quick enough for Max, who smacked it in the back and then Ismael's stick came down on its head!

We disposed of the rat in the burning hole and slept for the little night-time that remained. Most of us refused to use the bathroom for the rest of the weekend; consequently the bus trip back was a lot smellier than the first one!

I prayed very hard during this night and I can only thank the Lord no one got hurt (in fact, a lot more people got hurt in the swimming pool!)

Zak Datson – aged 15

It's not always hard work at boarding school, as you can see from Zak's story! Zak attends Bourofaye Christian School in Senegal while his parents are serving God in another country.

They banged on the windows and doors, and pointed their guns at us. 'Show us your passports!'

When the police demanded to see our passports, our friends realised they had forgotten to bring theirs. Now it looked like they might keep us in the police station all night! I was concerned about what the police might do to Dad.

Thankfully, Dad was able to talk with the police, and as we read the signs again we realised that we had actually reached the border! That explained why the police were annoyed. We were more than 100 km from where we should have been, having taken a wrong turn a couple of hours earlier.

The journey home was a little tense. Everyone was shaken after the experience and the younger kids started fighting a bit. We finally arrived home at around nine o'clock, exhausted after such an eventful day but thanking God that he had brought us back safely. And with a good story to tell.

Ruth Bateson – aged 12

For six-and-a-half years Ruth's family lived and worked in an arid part of Central Asia. They were thankful for God's guidance and protection – even when they got lost! Ruth would like to be a teacher in an international boarding school in India when she grows up.

Capsized

When I was about four my family moved to the Congo, 1000 miles from Kinshasa, the capital city.

Our lifestyle was very simple, there were no stores so we depended on local people coming to the house to sell us local produce like wild boar, and fruit grown in the forest. Others would bring eggs, and occasionally, honey. Our drinking water was collected from a spring, and wood for cooking was collected from the forest.

We were home-schooled by Mum and spent most of our geography classes daydreaming about what holidays we wanted to take. Then one day we decided that we should actually go away. Unfortunately, our destination was not as exotic as we had dreamed ... we were going by boat to another Congolese village for some rest and relaxation.

We packed our prettiest dresses and favourite toys, then climbed into an old, wooden boat and set off. It was a long trip, so we passed the time by pretending to fish. The first day of our journey was uneventful, and as the sun set, we found a village where we could stay overnight.

On the second day, after a short while, we began to see dark clouds in the distance. This could only mean one thing: a storm was brewing. Usually tropical storms are exciting. The smell in the air changes, it gradually gets windier and the sky darkens in a dramatic fashion until, all of a sudden, the heavens open and the rain comes beating down.

With little warning, a thunderstorm hit us. Rain fell suddenly like a waterfall, and a violent wind arrived; the boat immediately overturned and eighteen-foot high waves came over us. I found myself submerged in the murky, dark waters.

This would probably be a good time to tell you that many exotic animals live in these tropical rivers, including crocodiles. I couldn't swim and was trapped underneath the boat, with my head inching closer to the propeller. Luckily, my mother grabbed me, otherwise I would have been minced up. Shudder.

As I surfaced, the boat was overturned but did not sink because it was kept afloat by an empty barrel that was trapped underneath. However, the barrel could dislodge at any moment, taking the boat to its watery grave, and us with it.

Meanwhile, in England (where it was probably also raining), my grandmother was sitting down to her third coffee of the morning, when she instinctively knew something was wrong with our family. Something very wrong. Thousands of miles away, there was nothing to do but pray. And pray she did.

We managed to clamber on top of the capsized boat. As the rain continued to beat down, and the waves crashed over us, we were very aware that this could be the end for us. With our wet clothes clinging to us, all my sister and I could say was, 'Mummy, Daddy, we don't want to die'.

Rather than confirming our worst fears, my mum and dad suggested that we sing worship songs instead. This may seem a ridiculous idea but at this point we had nothing to lose. As my mum and dad later put it, if we were going to go down, then we were going to go down singing.

We saw one of our Bibles in the water, and my mum grabbed it, thinking God wanted to give us some last words of comfort and promise. With hope, she randomly opened up the Bible ... to the story of Jonah and the Big Fish. We were less than impressed!

After clinging to the top of this boat for four hours, the winds died down and the rains stopped, but we continued to drift along aimlessly, dreading the moment when the sun would finally go down and we would be all alone in the black river.

This is where I draw a blank. The next thing I remember is it being dark, and us emerging from the river onto dry land. We went to our friend's house, and they put us in dry clothes and gave us food.

In the days, weeks and months after the 'boat accident' we dried our Bibles, enrolled in swimming lessons and eventually the nightmares subsided.

To this day, fifteen years later, as a family we are aware that it was our heavenly Father who saved us that day, and we remain grateful that Jesus heard our prayers and worship and kept us safe.

This verse was given to us, which serves as a reminder that our God is bigger and more powerful than even the fiercest storm:

'Do not be afraid for I have reclaimed you,
I have called you by name, you are mine.
When you go through the sea, I am with you
When you go through the rivers, they will not sweep you away ...
I am the Lord your God, the Holy One of Israel,
your Saviour.'[1]

Jade Beakhouse

Jade is now living in Leeds, UK, studying for a Degree in Theology. She is torn between teaching and owning the best cake shop around!

---

[1] Isaiah 43:1-3 (God's Word Translation)

God's Care

Tia Anne is another kind of a granny, because she is not a real one, but she is like a granny to me. She used to live here, opposite my house but now she is in Singapore. I can't describe how Singapore looks because I haven't been there so I won't tell you. I miss her and also miss going to her house to play, and watching DVDs, and the biscuits and the juice she gave me and my brother, Daniel.

Hum mm ... do you wish you had three grannies? Well, I had two grannies, but then I chose Tia Anne to be my other granny, so maybe you can choose another granny for you too.

Lydia Honman – aged 6

Lydia was born in Brazil, but has lived in England with her parents and little brother, Daniel, since she was nine weeks old. She loves reading, writing and colouring. Lydia loves Jesus and has a very friendly and lively personality!

Pebble in a Stream

On a cold and chilly February day, my family and I arrived in China. I struggled with the weather: snow which was polluted by the dirty coal factories and air that was as thick as concrete! I was so tired, because of the nine-hour plane ride, that my back hurt. I woke up shrieking because I had a nightmare.

Experiencing culture shock at a young age is very difficult. Learning the alien language and culture of the Chinese was not an easy task for me. But living with the Chinese allowed me to taste new kinds of food. I learned that about 80 per cent of the food is fried. Also, the Chinese love hot spicy flavors.

At first, everything was unclear to me. Do the Chinese have brain calculators? How do they memorize so efficiently with such a short time? These queries were unravelled as I matured mentally and physically. The Chinese are a race that must not be underestimated. They have astute minds. I have seen Chinese children work hard, therefore they get the good results they deserve.

As an elementary student, my Chinese classmates would come to me and ask 'Do you want to play ball with us?' But I would frown with annoyance, which would scare them away. Years later, I strongly off your shoe. And if you didn't get the whole insect, sometimes the other half continued to run! The best thing was to take a flipflop, make a good hit, and give the dead insect to the cat to eat.

One time when I was using the bathroom before going to bed, I took a small kerosene lamp and placed it on the cement floor somewhere in front of our squat toilet. A roll of toilet paper was next to me on a big nail in the wall. I reached for the paper and wanted to pull off a piece. But the roll didn't move. I yanked a bit harder, but still I couldn't roll off the paper.

'Strange', I thought, 'it feels like something is stuck inside the roll'. I had no idea what that might have been. And then my feet froze to the ground. In the dim light of the kerosene lamp I saw something fat and black beginning to crawl out of the toilet paper roll. A spider!

I was so scared I couldn't move. What if that spider ran across to me squatting there? No one was there to help me. I was all alone. Alone with that fat, black spider. What should I do?

'Lord Jesus, please help me', I cried desperately in my heart.

And God was there with me in that poorly lit bathroom. He cared enough for the fears of a young girl to tell that spider to stay put. He made sure that it remained inside the roll until I was safely off the toilet and out of the room. Even spiders have to obey the God who is in control of everything.

Esther (Hornemann) Freudenberg

After finishing High School, Esther trained as a nurse, then served with WEC in the Gambia for a year. She loved sharing the Bible with school children. Today, Esther, with her husband and four children, still loves sharing the Bible with Sunday School children in Osnabruck, Germany.

Joe-Joe and Tailor

I'm Joe-Joe and my life is just one big adventure. I've been to about a dozen different countries, but you

sticks.

We also had two rabbits in a two-storey rabbit hutch. Once, the hutch door was left open and Tailor snuck into it. I came out and couldn't see the rabbits. All I could see was Tailor munching away at something. I jumped into it and saw Bobtail and Lofty (our rabbits) sitting petrified in the corner watching Tailor eating their vegetables, I picked him up and put him back on the ground then shut the cage door.

Thanks for reading my stories.

Joe-Joe – aged 11

It doesn't matter where you live, or what challenges you face, you can count on God to be there with you. Joe-Joe and his family have lived for ten years in a land that has known much war. His pets help to keep life normal! Joe-Joe would like to be a musician, a teacher or a doctor when he grows up.

Taking 'The Flamenco' to Holland

I remember very clearly the smells of the car engine, of the land in the evening, the taste of the rubber nozzle on the inflating air mattresses, the warm summer temperature, the touch of the tall grass on our bare legs. I remember the thrill of an unknown location in the middle of a forest, the animal sounds, and waking up in the silence broken by the birds.

My parents are Dutch but I was born and raised in Spain. In the past, when people asked if I felt Spanish or Dutch I would say, 'a little of both.' Recently I came up with a more specific answer. Now I say: 'I feel European. That is, I feel a little from everywhere. Quite Spanish, a little Dutch, a little English ... A citizen of the world!'

Every two years my family drove to Holland, crossing through Spain, France and Belgium. The trip was fantastic! We would prepare my father's big car, making a bed in the back for us to lie on during the trip (seat belts were not required!) My father sometimes took smaller roads and stopped by beautiful places in the countryside. All four siblings would put up the tent, while my mother prepared dinner and my father worked on the car.

When we visited supporting churches my father preached, my mother talked about their work in Spain and we would sing a Spanish song or perform a sketch. My little brother loved shouting his name into the microphone, which always made the people laugh and I remember teaching a whole church how to dance flamenco.

Being the son of Christian workers has its advantages and disadvantages. We moved many times, and I went to six different schools! I had to say 'bye' to many friends, and don't know what it is to have roots in a place. But I also adapt very well to new circumstances and new people. Being flexible and able to understand cultural differences has helped me a lot in my new job working with tourists.

Also, the treasure of falling in love with Jesus at a young age is priceless. I remember the warmth of the Jesus figurines on a flannel board, which my mother used to illustrate Bible stories. I remember my childhood escapes to the forest and how I would sing invented songs of praise to God. I remember the baptism of the Holy Spirit at nine years of age at a conference in Austria and the sheer joy I felt.

Now, as I think of Jesus it gives me such a sense of intimacy, of being at home. I thank God that my parents showed me the way.

Joel de Bruine

Joel is now the dad of two boys. He has two jobs, working for an air company, and tour guiding groups of US and Canadian students visiting Spain and France. Joel, as a church elder, is involved, with his wife, in family counselling. And ... he is also a singer in a rock band!

Monkeys, Rainstorms and War

'A pet monkey! We're getting a pet monkey?' Jeremy, Julianne and I shrieked.

I was fourteen years old, with large brown eyes and shoulder-length, caramel-coloured hair. Jeremy was two years younger than me and had mischievous blue eyes and short brown hair.

'Well, it's not a monkey, it's an olive baboon from Guinea,' explained Dad, 'and it's a gift to Julianne.'

My sister, Julianne, was the youngest. She had blue eyes, and a heavy sprinkling of freckles across her nose and cheeks. Julianne looked dubiously at the tiny baby baboon that was being held out to her. The baboon was officially given to her, but we all ended up sharing him.

Bilbo, the baboon, had velvety black fingers and toes, a fluffy brown coat, long tail, and light-blue eyelids. He was magnificent!

One of my favourite things to do in Liberia was to hold Bilbo on my lap and sit on the green porch wall during loud thunderstorms! Africa has amazing rainstorms. Can you imagine how much noise rain would make if it was falling onto a metal roof? It is like a beautiful drum show over your head.

Sometimes it got lonely being in Africa. I loved making new friends, but sometimes I missed my American friends, and familiar American things like running water and electricity. God was so sweet though! Just when I was feeling most homesick, God made the electricity come on—right on my birthday! Plus we had several new Lebanese and African friends come over to celebrate my birthday.

Around Christmas time a civil war broke out in Liberia. Pretty soon people in our town started loading all their belongings (beds, dressers, clothes and buckets) onto pick-up trucks and moving away. We were afraid at times and wondered what would happen next.

In my journal, I wrote about the stress of seeing people leave:

> *Our yard is silent and empty. The quiet, fear and unrest are playing on everyone's emotions. People snap at each other. Frowns are on everyone's faces. Eyes shift nervously. Murmuring and grumbling starts and then fades away.*

> *Frustration is on the wind. You can see it on the face of a wailing babe – its mother is gone, and the other siblings are out of hearing range. You can see it written on the boarded up windows and doors of once noisy homes.*

> *It's running down the cheeks of a dusty girl. It's in the racking cough of an old man left in an empty house. It's wrapped around the sobbing, lonely woman standing in the middle of a deserted road with her belongings scattered around her.*

It's in this room, hanging over my shoulder. It's coursing down my cheeks. It's in my sobs, blending in with the song on the radio.

As a family, we prayed together a lot, wondering what we should do. Soon the United States government helped us make our decision—all Americans were ordered to leave Liberia. But where would we go? What should we pack?

The planes were all full and wouldn't have spots for us for several weeks, plus the war was getting closer. News reports said the airports may be shut down soon for good.

'God, what should we do?' we asked. I packed my red backpack, we said goodbye to Bilbo, and we waited to see what God would do. In my journal, I wrote:

All airlines to the States and Europe are reserved up through May. We couldn't humanly leave this continent if we wanted to! We were busy packing all yesterday. It's hard to decide what to leave here when there's a chance we may never see it again!

Sunday, May 6th, 1990
After running around and last minute re-packing, we raced to the airport yesterday, still not knowing if we would actually leave since we were on standby.

Three hours later the plane took off and we were on it! God is so wonderful! We prayed for the right papers, for transportation, to be able to get on the plane, and for our ears not to hurt. God answered every single one of them.

Jennifer (Pinke) Dougan

Jennifer and her pastor husband, Mark, now work together with students at their church near Minneapolis. Their three children, aged 3 to 16 years, love to hear stories about their mum's pet baboon, Bilbo. Jennifer is a writer and speaker, working to publish her book about the civil war in Liberia.

God's Surprises

God and a Burger Bar

I didn't want to move, no matter what my mum and dad said!

Sometimes living in Asia can be hard. Especially when God tells my mum and dad what he wants them to do and I don't want to do it. This is what happened when my parents believed that God was saying our family should move to another town.

I really did not want to move there. So I asked God for something to prove to me we should move. I told God I did not want to go unless there was a burger bar (never seen in this country) and something I liked, like football or Dr Who. I didn't think God could answer that.

When we went to the other town for the visit I was really bored. It was okay for a holiday, but I didn't want to live there.

On the last day we met friends from another town and guess where they took us for lunch – a newly-opened burger bar! I couldn't believe it. It was outrageous. After a yummy burger we decided to go to the park.

For a God reason we couldn't get a bus. Then I saw it: a whole tiny shop selling football stuff. Not only football stuff but Liverpool stuff – my favourite team. It was the best day and now I don't mind going there. God answered me.

Since then my town has had an earthquake. Sadly, many buildings have gone, but the burger bar survived and it is still selling burgers.

Caleb Vonk – aged 11

Caleb loves football, burgers and Dr Who. He and his family have lived in a fairly remote, mountainous region of Asia for about five years. I wonder how many people in this region know that they, like Caleb, are important to God.

God Knew

'Foreign Christian teenagers *leave* this country for schooling, they don't come to *live!'*

I was worried. I have lived in the Middle East since I was three. An extrovert, I always like to be with people, and God had given me three lovely Christian friends my age. But that year all of them were planning to leave the country and go back home.

The year before, two men visited our city to see if God wanted them to bring their families and move here. Dad had been their 'guide'. One of these men had a boy eleven years old, the same age as my brother, and a girl thirteen years old – my age! I was excited and I gave him my e-mail address to give to his daughter so we could get to know each other before they came.

I waited and waited, but she didn't write. 'Maybe she's just shy,' I said. But after a few months I knew that wasn't the problem. 'What if she didn't want to be my friend?', I thought. Time went by and soon I forgot about it.

As the time drew near when the family would come, I began to think about the girl again. I was worried, but I also hung onto hope. Then I found out that their arrival time had been put off by a few months. 'What if they don't come at all?' I wondered.

The worries came back. 'Will I be all alone with no one to hang out with?' Yes, I do have local friends, but it is different around them. Even though I speak the language well, our cultures are very different.

When I 'hang out' with my expat friends we get creative because we grew up learning to be creative. But the local girls were not taught that when they were young. Being creative and just goofing around is something very new to them.

I also wanted someone who could relate to me, who went through the same cultural issues as me and who, most of all, knew the Lord.

This time, the family's arrival date stayed the same. 'Maybe they will come after all?' I thought. And sure enough, they did. The thirteen-year-old girl and I became close friends. It turned out that the note I had sent her had been lost, so she couldn't write to me!

Now she lives two houses down the road, we see each other almost every day and I can walk to her house by myself. If she lived any further away I could only walk there if accompanied by my brothers or my parents. In this country young women don't wander around the streets alone.

When I go over to her place we listen to music, talk, goof around, dance, sew, crochet, watch movies and we have a lot of sleep-overs on the weekends. God is good! He knew they would come. He knew I needed a friend. I begin to see that I should never have doubted or worried, because God knew!

Emma Clarke – aged 13

Emma and her family have lived in the Middle East for ten years, and are thankful for all that God has done for them. In the Bible, God says, 'I will answer them before they even call to me. While they are still talking to me about their needs, I will go ahead and answer their prayers![1]

Can you think of a time when God did something special for you?

---

[1] Isaiah 65:24

The Whisper of God

Our family of five did everything together in Japan. House to house visitation brought offers to come inside as the people wanted to see the fair-haired babies up close. Mum and Dad had to work hard to keep us from being spoilt.

We went to Japanese Nursery School and were then home schooled. We loved it! It was great always being the top of the class. Unfortunately, we were also at the bottom of the class.

Summer camps were held every year as an outreach to the Japanese people. My sisters and I went along with Mum and Dad to help.

I was about twelve years old when Mum was working in the kitchen and Dad was the shopper for a camp for 14-16 year olds. I volunteered to help as 'odd jobs man' – boiling water and cooling it for drinking, fetching this and that, a dogsbody of sorts but I enjoyed it.

The campers were having a curry bar-b-q on the beach. As there were some extra sausages I was asked to take them to the five groups. At the fifth group someone offered the last sausage to me. We played paper-scissors-rock to see who would win it.

The Golden Chariot

Just as I won I had a terrible pain in my ear. It was enough to bring tears to my eyes.

I went to Mum and she sent me to the camp nurse who listened and checked the ear, but could see nothing. She wondered if, perhaps, a spark from the fire had flown into it and suggested putting in some olive oil. While she went to the kitchen to warm the oil Mum and I waited. Mum suggested we pray. When I prayed, I asked God, 'Please help the oil to be effective and to heal the pain.'

By the time the nurse returned the pain had subsided. I was given the choice of having the oil in any case or just forgetting it. We were about to leave it when Mum remembered my prayer and said, 'Since no harm could come by using the oil it might be best to put it in'. I lay on the bed, the oil went in and out came a baby centipede!

How glad we were that we had listened to the whisper of the spirit of God and to find the nasty creature flushed out rather than leaving it to attack again.

Tomi Owens

Have you ever heard God's whisper? Has he helped you to make a good decision? Tomi now has three children and is a pastor, as well as head of the Maths Department in a girls' school in Jersey, Channel Islands. In 2002 he took his wife and baby daughter to Japan to show them his 'roots'.

Boiled Cabbage

I don't remember how old I was when I discovered that I actually like boiled cabbage.

I was at Vavoua International School, a boarding school nestled in the elephant grass of Côte d'Ivoire in West Africa. The school did their best to provide us with good meals, but of course there were things that we didn't want to eat. Liver was high on that list, and so was spinach.

The rules said we had to take some of everything that was on the table, and we had to eat everything that was on our plate. So we did, but we weren't always happy about it.

I don't know why we didn't like boiled cabbage. It just sounded like something kids are supposed to not like, so we didn't.

Then one day I sat down to a lunch which included boiled cabbage. I took my cabbage like a good girl and ate it first, saving the best for last. I don't remember what 'the best' was, but we had great meals like rice with peanut sauce and alloco (fried plantain bananas), and oodles of mangos and bananas and papayas for dessert.

So, of course, I ate the nasty cabbage quickly and enjoyed the yummy food after it. And then I asked someone to please pass the cabbage, and took seconds.

'Wait! What are you doing!?!?!?!' said my brain.

'But it tastes good,' replied my brain.

'It does?' My brain asked back.

'Yes, it does.'

'Oh. You're right, it does! I wonder why I thought I didn't like it.'

All that happened in a split second, and I realized I like boiled cabbage.

You would think I would have learned from the cabbage, but the same thing happened with Grandma's rhubarb jam. Rhubarb didn't grow in Côte d'Ivoire, so I classed it with other weirdly named vegetables I had never tasted (like asparagus and cauliflower). Then once, when we were in the US, I tried Grandma's rhubarb jam, not knowing that it was rhubarb – it was delicious! (Cauliflower is good too, but I still don't like asparagus.)

Food isn't the only thing I've missed out on. When God created the world, he put SO MANY amazing, weird, beautiful, bizarre things into it. I don't know how he thought of them all, but I'm glad he did. They are God's gifts to us. I love the feel of wind blowing the rains after a long dry season, the colours of a bushfire, and the smell of fresh cookies.

Some other gifts I refused to thank God for: I survived several winters of misery before I saw beauty in sparkling snow! Now I can thank God for the snow (and for letting me live in Africa so I wouldn't be cold all the time).

God is teaching me to see His fingerprints of beauty in many things (and even people) I don't like. When I see (or hear or feel) the beauty, it's easier to live with them. Sometimes I even end up liking them!

Joelle Durben

Joelle is now a teacher for kids growing up in other countries like she did, and gets to live in whatever country the kids live in. She loves her cat, reading, cooking, and discovering the awesome world God has given us!

We had to leave Guinea-Bissau because of the war. I lived in my home country, Germany, for eleven years. After I graduated from high school I felt that God wanted to send me back to Africa, this time to Senegal, to BCS the Missionary kids school. I worked there for one year as a dorm helper, teaching German and Geography and taking care of the children.

During that time it was always my wish to return to Guinea-Bissau and see my old place and Tibna again. At Easter I had everything planned and sorted out. But Guinea Bissau had political problems and my flight was cancelled. I didn't get the money back and I was so disappointed. It probably wouldn't be possible ever again. I was mad at God, the government – just everything.

But then God surprised me again. Tibna was able to come to BCS because of a family who works for WEC. It was like a dream when I met him again. We couldn't talk without help any more because his English wasn't very good and I'd forgotten all my Portuguese and Creole. But we felt like friends again.

Now, as I sit in front of this computer and think back to the time I had, it fills my heart with thankfulness. Thank you God for being amazing.

Jana Böker – aged 19

Many TCKs, after they return to their home country, have a great longing to return to the land of their childhood. God gave Jana this wonderful opportunity. She is now studying acting in Germany and would love to combine acting with missionary work.

The Old Kerosene Fridge

The old kerosene fridge was dead. Having endured many moves in Java, it had finally decided enough was enough. It sat very still in its corner of the kitchen. No amount of coaxing could bring that spark of life back into it.

They say that kerosene fridges, especially old ones, are like elderly ladies. They hum along very happily if left in one location. But they don't like change. And they seriously object to many changes.

Dad had spent the morning working patiently with the old fridge. He had cleaned and relit the wick, but the flame did not spring into life. Now it was time to return to Wonogiri to pick up the rest of the furniture. He shook his head as he said to Mum, 'This time I think it really has gone. We'll have to pray about getting a new one. They are very expensive. I guess we'll have to wait a while.' Then he was off.

Michie and Meg looked at the fridge. 'When Jesus laid his hands on people they got better. Could we lay hands on our fridge and pray for it?' they asked Mum. 'Let's do it', said Mum. So the three of them gathered around the fridge. Little Andy toddled up and joined them, placing his chubby hands on the fridge. Together they asked Jesus to bring the old fridge back to life.

God's Love

Ferry Crossing

The sound of wheels spinning caught my attention. The back wheel of a large van had got stuck over the edge of the ferry ramp and was in the water. The wheel kept spinning and the rest of the van was starting to slide towards the water ...

My parents worked in a small country called Guinea-Bissau. We would often travel by ferry, across large rivers, to visit the neighbouring countries of Gambia and Senegal. Back then my understanding of what a ferry trip involved was quite different to my experience now of British ferries!

One day, after a long, hot drive, we finally arrived at the ferry crossing, along with many other people. My heart sank as I realised we would be waiting for a while behind queues of vehicles – in the heat, with little shade and lots of flies.

To pass the time, I walked down to the jetty, passing small huts selling food and drink which smelled really delicious, especially the large hunks of meat and the bags of iced juice. People bustled past me, some running, others walking in groups, some with children and some dragging animals. There was a loud volume of chatter, arguments and shouting from one side of the road to the other, not to mention the bleating and squawking of animals.

As I stood up on the riverbank overlooking the deep, brown, muddy river I watched rubbish float by and could see our destination in the distance: a wooden shack and lots of people. Next to me people were washing their feet, animals were drinking and children were pulling plastic bags and old flipflops from the dirty water.

With excitement I watched the ferry come closer and could hear the noise level rise. Everyone and everything started moving and calling to one another in hope that, after hours of waiting, they would finally get across. Finally, the old, oily and very tired-looking ferry arrived, crammed full – and chaos erupted.

People were running and barging their way off, trying to dodge the vehicles also trying to get off the ferry. There were tall women dressed in brightly coloured, long-flowing dresses. Some had babies tied onto their backs, others carried big bags on their heads. There were some smartly dressed men, others in long white tunics and a few in shabby, dirty clothes also added to the chaos. I didn't notice the children; it was the fantastically dressed women that caught my eye.

Among the few posh 4x4s there were old, tattered-looking vehicles piled high with bags, sacks of rice and animals on their roofs. My eyes half closed as I watched these unbalanced vehicles wobbling as the drivers tried to manoeuvre them. Due to low tide the ferry ramp hadn't met the jetty properly, which meant

that cars were scraping their bumpers and oil tanks on their way up the slope.

The sound of wheels spinning caught my attention. The back wheel of a large van had got stuck over the edge of the ramp and was in the water. The wheel kept spinning and the rest of the van was starting to slide towards the water. People were shouting, trying to pull and push the van back onto the ramp and up onto the jetty. This lasted a good fifteen minutes.

I didn't watch the next part for fear, instead I prayed that God would help them to get out and up the ramp. After what seemed like an age there was a screech of tyres and the van shot up the jetty, nearly hitting a few passengers on its way up.

At last the ferry was empty, so I took a deep breath and a gulp as I waited for our car to be driven on, praying that we would be looked after, that the ferry would stay in one piece and that we would arrive on the other side before night time.

I praise God for His continued faithfulness and protection of my family.

Ruth Whitehorn

People are on God's heart. That's why, after 14 years in Africa, Ruth's desire was to help people. Now studying in the UK, Ruth would like to work as a Social Worker when she completes her Masters degree.

The Miracle

Calling friends from other parts of the country to visit before someone dies is part of the culture in Pakistan.

One day we heard that Asif was sick with kidney failure. He was the older uncle of a Christian family we knew. He had been admitted to his local hospital and was in the intensive care unit on a life support machine.

The hospitals in Pakistan aren't that posh. You never know what creatures, creepy-crawlies and diseases could be hiding in the shadows. Even the doctors aren't always 100 per cent qualified.

Asif's family were praying for him from the moment he went into hospital. But after a few days on the life support machine the doctors realised the treatment was not working. The doctors advised Asif's son to invite all the relatives and close friends to come and say 'goodbye' to him.

The relatives in the north of the country had to buy train tickets to travel to the city where Asif was. The tickets were a lot of money for them. They were not the richest of families and it was not easy for them to find the money. When they did get the tickets the journey took them around two days.

On the day the doctors were going to turn off the life support machine, the relatives gathered round to see Asif for the last time. So they said their last words of appreciation to him ...

The doctors turned off the life support machine ...

But after a while Asif sat up on the bed he had been lying on. Everyone was amazed!

A few days later he was moved out of the intensive care unit into a normal ward. Asif's family could hardly believe what was happening. The doctors were as surprised as everyone else.

Asif continued to get better. Eventually he was able to go home, and the relatives from the north of the country went home too. Up until now he is still alive and going well.

Joel – aged 11

The story reminds me of the Bible story of Lazarus[1] who got more and more sick, and even died. But just when his family had given up hope, Jesus healed him! Would you like to pray for the people of Pakistan, that many more of them will come to know this wonder-working God?

---

[1] John 11:1-44

Village on the Amazon

As small children we lived with our parents in an indigenous tribe in northern Amazon. We were fascinated by their culture and how they lived and talked.

In the village we played with the children: singing children's rhymes, plaiting each other's hair, making sand castles. But what we most liked to do was to watch the sunset and stay until early evening watching the stars with our father and mother in front of our house.

We would bathe ourselves in the river and when it rained a lot we bathed at home with a bucket. The water was so cold in the river!

Once when we were coming back to the city, we had no place to stay for the night, so we stopped the boat at an island. That night we were so tired that we didn't set up the hammock. We just slept on the rocks by the riverside. Often in the middle of the night there are lots of ants who eat through the plastic that people sleep on, and through their sandals, but God helped us and nothing bad happened, and no snakes appeared. So next day when we woke up we went back to the city and arrived home safely.

One of our favourite things to do when we were in the village was to go into the forest with our dad and some of the local people. We made a lot of friends and, with our little knowledge of their language, we tried to tell them when we were playing that Jesus loved them.

Although the village on the Amazon wasn't always the nicest place for us children, and we sometimes missed our friends at home, we knew that it was where God wanted us and we obeyed him joyfully.

Marilis Schmidel – 13 years
Evelise Schmidel – 15 years

How special that Evelise and Marilis were able to tell their friends on the Amazon that Jesus loves them! Sometimes God leads his children to difficult places so that people there have opportunity to hear the Good News. Evelise would like to do this when she grows up. Marilis wants to be a doctor ... or a crime scene investigator!

Who Wouldn't Eat Rat Stew!

Have you ever smelt burning rat's hair? Let me warn you now – don't! It's the most disgusting, revolting, foul smell ever. You may by now be wondering how I know this small, insignificant, gross fact. Well, the knowledge behind it is part of a funny scene in our back garden about ten years ago.

It was almost midday and a group of village ladies sat with my mum under a mango tree, shading themselves from the glaring sun. Then all of a sudden a gigantic rat scampered across the garden, shooting out of nowhere across the sand. Without hesitation the ladies leapt to their feet, grabbing the closest weapons they could lay their hands on.

I must point out that it's a very amusing sight for a five-year-old to see grown women running chaotically with shovels and sticks after an overgrown rodent. However, you must be aware that in Gambia, finding a rat is like finding a free meal, especially when it's bigger than most over-fed cats.

Cornered helplessly behind the shed, the rat scrambled desperately back into an empty pipe, hopefully safe from these wild women and their weapons. Close to triumph, the ladies called over my bewildered mum, signaling for her to lift up the opposite end of the long, plastic pipe. The prediction was that by lifting one end, the rat would plop out the other, where they would be ready to brutally bash it on the head.

Unexpectedly, my mum got the shock of her life when a long, rubbery tail, followed by a large, hairy bum, wriggled suddenly from the top of the pipe, almost into her surprised face.

Finally the rat was caught and without further ado, its hair singed off, polluting us all with rat stench. After skinning it, however, a problem occurred. Where could the rat be cooked? The look on my mum's face showed she had no intention of letting the kitchen be used to cook such a stinky animal, but after lots of persuasion she was forced to give in and saucepans where set up over the small gas rings. As the rat was gently prodded and stirred, a strong smell wafted through the house. Gradually the pan filled as first they asked for an onion, then an OXO cube and then a carrot or two until the stew bubbled with perfection.

Satisfied and happy, and thankful to God for his provision, the ladies sat down to devour their steaming rodent platter while I watched rather nervously from a distance.

Later that afternoon Dad returned home to be welcomed by a bowl of the glorious concoction and a house stinking of rat. Slightly put off by the smell, he declined the offer. I mean, who wouldn't eat rat stew?

Abigail – aged 15

What is your favourite meal? Ever tried Rat Stew?? Abi's parents have been involved in medical work in The Gambia for many years. Abi and her sister, Lydia, attend Bourafaye Christian School, a boarding school in Senegal. Some funny things happen when they are home!

Reflections

In the tall yellow field of grass and bamboo I sat, a young girl in Indonesia, clutching a new plastic Barbie doll. It was getting close to Christmas and this was my special gift – sent early from Australia where they were all the rage.

I studied her intently – smooth white skin, painted blue eyes and long blonde hair – blonde as my own. She looked so foreign, so strange. A visitor to an alien land. I'd never had a Barbie doll before.

Out in the paddy fields, during the midday break, when the sun burnt the land, I had sat under a coconut tree with my Javanese friends and learned how to make a doll. Nimble brown fingers carefully tore the long, green sugar cane leaves into strips and I watched as they folded and twisted and tied a doll. I copied too – but had made many such dolls, and I threw them away when they got old. Beside my Barbie they were so pitiful.

It was getting hot in my little field and I could feel my pale skin burning. I searched the sky for signs of the coming rain. I loved the monsoons. As they approached the sticky, wet heat grew heavy and almost unbearable. Then, finally, the sweet smell of wet dust and far-off rain.

By afternoon it would be upon us – falling in huge hard droplets on every street and house. We'd scream with excitement, and tear off barefoot with our friends to play in the rain and run along the streets and cake ourselves with mud from splashing in every puddle – just for the sheer enjoyment of the rain.

I could hear the kids playing with the monkey in the house next door. The babble of Bahasa Indonesia and Javanese floated easily across. I wondered what the kids in Australia played? Did they like running in the rain? What did they look like? I could hardly remember – like me, I guessed.

Mum and Dad had mentioned that we might have to go there soon. That's what made me start thinking. In ten years time would I remember this moment? Could I picture the tall yellow fields where I sat? Would my priorities change? Would I change?

We left before the rains came. And I miss the monsoons. Of course I discovered what Australian kids play with instead. I had three more new Barbie dolls within the month. I've given them all away now – they seem so pitiful.

I keep trying to remember Indonesia, reliving the memories so that I don't lose them forever. But it's getting harder. All I can recall well are the moments where I'd sat in the wild open fields and wondered, 'will I remember this some day?'

Sometimes Indonesia seems as unreal as a picture or a far-off dream. But I love to remember the hot golden fields and little brown bodies and the exhilaration of running barefoot in the rain.

Megan (Kallmier) Kearnes – written when she was 15

After she returned to Australia, and completed university, Megan worked as a lawyer for refugees from many countries. She now loves being a mum to two little girls, and sharing about God's love for people from every country.

Good News in Bandit Country

'That area is full of bandits,' the motor mechanic said, 'If I go there I might get robbed!' But there were children waiting to hear good news.

Our convoy of cars full of Christian workers and Thai believers had been travelling over the dangerous Thai mountains on the way to a wedding. The surrounding forest looked beautiful as the sun peeked through the leaves of the trees. In the back of the pick-up truck the Thai people were all joyful and happy despite the long journey. Someone had brought a camera with them and pictures were taken constantly.

Suddenly, a noise came from the front of the car. We looked up to see a cloud of black smoke come out of the engine. Quickly the car was stopped and everyone jumped out motioning the other cars to stop too. Everyone was worried. 'What's wrong with the car? Is it going to blow up?' It soon became obvious that the car would not start up again and it looked like we were going to be stuck on the hill for a while.

A couple of people decided to go off to the nearest town in one of the cars while the rest of us waited. They found a mechanic. However, he refused to come and fix the car when he was told where the car was. 'That area is full of bandits,' he said, 'If I go there I might get robbed!' They suddenly became worried as they realized that they had left everyone else behind in a dangerous area where they could easily be robbed!

Back in the mountains we tried to get comfortable, wondering what we were going to do for an hour or so. Many looked for some sort of shade to escape from the blistering hot sun. The area around was very quiet and it seemed as if no one lived nearby at all. Thick forest surrounded one side of the road and on the other side was a steep drop down the mountain. We were all completely unaware that they were in an area full of bandits!

Suddenly out of the bushes came some shy but inquisitive tribal children. They had spirit strings tied around their thin wrists to protect them from evil spirits and wore ragged clothing. They came over to where some of us were sitting, curious as to why we were all there.

They were staring particularly at the white people in our group – commonly known as 'farangs'. They hadn't seen a white person before! We smiled at the children and called out, 'Pay nay?' which is a Thai greeting meaning, 'Where are you going?'

As the children came nearer some of the adults suddenly remembered about the conference that they had just come from. They had all been given materials to use for sharing Jesus with children and one person, Wichian, still had a wordless book in his pocket. He asked the children, 'Do you want to hear a special story?' They replied, 'Yes,' in Thai and came over to listen. Wichian chatted to them and using the colourful book, taught them the Good News about Jesus.

An hour passed quickly and eventually a willing mechanic was found and brought back to fix the car. Soon we were back on the road and on our way to the wedding. It was only when we were in the car that we were told about the fact that the area was full of dangerous bandits!

I was amazed that God not only kept us safe but He had also given us the opportunity to share the gospel with the children.

Luke Parkes – aged 16

Would you like to pray for the Thai tribal children that they may come to know Jesus? Luke, with his family, lived in Thailand for many years. Now Luke is in his final years of high school in England. He would like to study medicine and serve God in overseas mission.

Danger in the Jungle

I once had a friend named Marcos. We grew up deep in the Amazon Rainforest of Colombia, South America. Our friends were the Indian children around us. We lived in a village in a thatched roof house with bark walls like the Indians.

My friend, Marcos, lived in another village not far from ours. He would often come over to our village and play with my brother, sisters and I. At a young age he accepted the Lord Jesus as his Saviour and would share with his family who Jesus was and what He meant to him. When my family went to his village he would gather all his family members around to listen to what my father shared about new life in Christ.

One day Marcos was walking on a jungle path with his younger brother and they came upon a poisonous snake and her nesting area. My friend saw it and reacted quickly by pushing his brother to safety. This snake sank her teeth and venom into my friend's thigh. She bit him twice. His little brother ran home to get his family, but when they got back it was too late.

A family member came to my father with the sad news and asked my father if he could construct a coffin. My father said, 'Yes, no problem.' He had just the material to make it with.

That afternoon as I walked down the jungle path I could feel the sadness radiating off my father. As I watched his large hands build the coffin he explained to me about death and the importance of having Christ as my Saviour. He explained to me about the death of my friend and how the coffin he was building was for his earthly body, but that he was on his way to be with Jesus.

The next morning, as I watched my dad get into the boat, his shoulders were slumped over in sadness for the family. As he dragged the coffin behind him, I understood what my dad was telling me the day before. I got on my knees and prayed for my friend's family.

That day Marcos' father asked my dad many questions about where his son was, did he feel pain now, how could he see him again as my dad said he might. Dad answered each of his questions, assuring him that in heaven there is no more pain, and no more sadness. He explained again salvation through Jesus. Marcos' dad said that he wanted to accept Jesus and he did right there with my father.

When my father left the house where Marcos' body was laid out he heard the women come back to the house and begin their wailing. Marcos' father quieted them and began telling them about Jesus. He later told my father that his family became Christians that day. My friend's death was for God's glory because God used his death to bring his family to Christ.

Rebecca (Dulka) O'Neill

We know that Jesus loves us so much he gave his life for us. Marcos loved his brother so much that he gave his life for his brother – and eventually for his whole family! His friend, Rebecca, is now married and has three beautiful daughters. She enjoys working in her local church with children who have special needs, and helping them to learn more about Jesus.

A Special Friend

The Bible says that the greatest love is shown when people give their lives for their friends (John 15:13). Just as Marcos gave his life for his little brother, Jesus gave his life for us. He loves us so much that he was willing to die for us. Jesus knew that was the only way to take away all the wrong things that get between us and God.

The Lord Jesus knows all about you and longs for you to ask him to be your friend! Tell him that you want to get rid of the bad stuff in your life. Then tell him you want to live his way and do what he wants you to do. You can be sure that he will help you!

Spend time getting to know your friend, Jesus. Talk with him – any time, any place. Read his book, the Bible, and learn special verses. God's Holy Spirit will help you to pray and live your life for Jesus.

What is WEC?

CT Studd, a famous cricketer, left his career to serve Christ in China and India. Then in 1913 he felt God calling him to pioneer a new mission. Passionate to see Africans worshipping Jesus, this 53-year-old man with poor health set sail for the heart of Africa. God turned this one man's crazy adventure into a mission and a movement that has since touched millions of lives.

WEC is now a huge Christian family! Around 1,800 workers, from many churches and over 50 nations, serve God in multicultural teams among 90 of the least evangelised people groups.

About one third of the world's population has never heard the stories of Jesus. They have never met a group of God's people. WEC's aim is to see Jesus known, loved and worshipped among these peoples.

God wants us to pray and to share with him in his work. When we pray for people in other countries we are working with God as he works in people's hearts.

WEC runs short and long-term programs for people wanting to serve God in other countries, and has six training centres around the world.

CT Studd, a famous cricketer, left his career to serve Christ in China and India. Then in 1913 he felt God calling him to pioneer a new mission. Passionate to see Africans worshipping Jesus, this 53-year-old man with poor health set sail for the heart of Africa. God turned this one man's crazy adventure into a mission and a movement that has since touched millions of lives.

WEC is now a huge Christian family! Around 1,800 workers, from many churches and over 50 nations, serve God in multicultural teams among 90 of the least evangelised people groups.

About one third of the world's population has never heard the stories of Jesus. They have never met a group of God's people. WEC's aim is to see Jesus known, loved and worshipped among these peoples.

God wants us to pray and to share with him in his work. When we pray for people in other countries we are working with God as he works in people's hearts.

WEC runs short and long-term programs for people wanting to serve God in other countries, and has six training centres around the world.

If you want to know more about WEC ... go to our international website www.wec-int.org and find the WEC website for your country.

WEC, working together with local churches, sends workers from Australia, Brazil, Canada, Finland, Fiji, France, Italy, Germany, Hong Kong, Indonesia, Korea, New Zealand, Singapore, South Africa, Switzerland, Taiwan, The Netherlands, UK and USA.

TRAILBLAZER SERIES

Martyn Lloyd-Jones, From Wales to Westminster
ISBN 978-1-85792-349-0

George Müller, The Children's Champion
ISBN 978-1-85792-549-4

Robert Murray McCheyne, Life is an Adventure
ISBN 978-1-85792-947-8

John Newton, A Slave Set Free
ISBN 978-1-85792-834-1

Mary of Orange, At the Mercy of Kings
ISBN 978-1-84550-818-0

John Paton, A South Sea Island Rescue
ISBN 978-1-85792-852-5

Helen Roseveare, On His Majesty's Service
ISBN 978-1-84550-259-1

Mary Slessor, Servant to the Slave
ISBN 978-1-85792-348-3

Charles Spurgeon, Prince of Preachers
ISBN 978-1-84550-155-6

Patricia St. John, The Story Behind the Stories
ISBN 978-1-84550-328-4

John Stott, The Humble Leader
ISBN 978-1-84550-787-9

Joni Eareckson Tada, Swimming against the Tide
ISBN 978-1-85792-833-4

Hudson Taylor, An Adventure Begins
ISBN 978-1-85792-423-7

John Welch, The Man who couldn't be Stopped
ISBN 978-1-85792-928-7

George Whitefield, The Voice that Woke the World
ISBN 978-1-84550-772-5

William Wilberforce, The Freedom Fighter
ISBN 978-1-85792-371-1

Richard Wurmbrand, A Voice in the Dark
ISBN 978-1-85792-298-1

Start collecting this series now!

Ten Boys who used their Talents:
ISBN 978-1-84550-146-4
Paul Brand, Ghillean Prance, C.S.Lewis,
C.T. Studd, Wilfred Grenfell, J.S. Bach,
James Clerk Maxwell, Samuel Morse,
George Washington Carver, John Bunyan.

Ten Girls who used their Talents:
ISBN 978-1-84550-147-1
Helen Roseveare, Maureen McKenna,
Anne Lawson, Harriet Beecher Stowe,
Sarah Edwards, Selina Countess of Huntingdon, Mildred Cable,
Katie Ann MacKinnon,
Patricia St. John, Mary Verghese.

Ten Boys who Changed the World:
ISBN 978-1-85792-579-1
David Livingstone, Billy Graham, Brother Andrew,
John Newton, William Carey, George Müller,
Nicky Cruz, Eric Liddell, Luis Palau,
Adoniram Judson.

Ten Girls who Changed the World:
ISBN 978-1-85792-649-1
Corrie Ten Boom, Mary Slessor,
Joni Eareckson Tada, Isobel Kuhn,
Amy Carmichael, Elizabeth Fry, Evelyn Brand, Gladys Aylward,
Catherine Booth, Jackie Pullinger.

Ten Boys who Made a Difference:
ISBN 978-1-85792-775-7
Augustine of Hippo, Jan Hus, Martin Luther,
Ulrich Zwingli, William Tyndale, Hugh Latimer,
John Calvin, John Knox, Lord Shaftesbury,
Thomas Chalmers.

Ten Girls who Made a Difference:
ISBN 978-1-85792-776-4
Monica of Thagaste, Catherine Luther,
Susanna Wesley, Ann Judson, Maria Taylor,
Susannah Spurgeon, Bethan Lloyd-Jones,
Edith Schaeffer, Sabina Wurmbrand,
Ruth Bell Graham.

Ten Boys who Made History:
ISBN 978-1-85792-836-5
Charles Spurgeon, Jonathan Edwards,
Samuel Rutherford, D L Moody,
Martin Lloyd Jones, A W Tozer, John Owen, Robert Murray
McCheyne, Billy Sunday,
George Whitfield.

Ten Girls who Made History:
ISBN 978-1-85792-837-2
Ida Scudder, Betty Green, Jeanette Li,
Mary Jane Kinnaird, Bessie Adams,
Emma Dryer, Lottie Moon, Florence Nightingale, Henrietta
Mears, Elisabeth Elliot.

Ten Boys who Didn't Give In:
ISBN 978-1-84550-035-1
Polycarp, Alban, Sir John Oldcastle
Thomas Cramer, George Wishart,
James Chalmers, Dietrich Bonhoeffer,
Nate Saint, Ivan Moiseyev,
Graham Staines.

Ten Girls who Didn't Give In:
ISBN 978-1-84550-036-8
Blandina, Perpetua, Lady Jane Grey,
Anne Askew, Lysken Dirks, Marion Harvey,
Margaret Wilson, Judith Weinberg,
Betty Stam, Esther John.

The Adventures Series
An ideal series to collect

Have you ever wanted to visit the Rainforest? Have you ever longed to sail down the Amazon river? Would you just love to go on Safari in Africa? Well these books can help you imagine that you are actually there.

Pioneer missionaries retell their amazing adventures and encounters with animals and nature. In the Amazon you will discover tree frogs, piranha fish and electric eels. In the Rainforest you will be amazed at the armadillo and the toucan. In the blistering heat of the African Savannah you will come across lions and elephants and hyenas. And you will discover how God is at work in these amazing environments.

Rainforest Adventures by Horace Banner
ISBN 978-1-85792-627-9

African Adventures by Dick Anderson
ISBN 978-1-85792-807-5

Amazon Adventures by Horace Banner
ISBN 978-1-85792-440-4

Cambodian Adventures by Donna Vann
ISBN 978-1-84550-474-8

Great Barrier Reef Adventures by Jim Cromarty
ISBN 978-1-84550-068-9

Himalayan Adventures by Penny Reeve
ISBN 978-1-84550-080-1

Kiwi Adventures by Bartha Hill
ISBN 978-1-84550-282-9

New York City Adventures by Donna Vann
ISBN 978-1-84550-546-2

Outback Adventures by Jim Cromarty
ISBN 978-1-85792-974-4

Pacific Adventures by Jim Cromarty
ISBN 978-1-84550-475-5

Rainforest Adventures by Horace Banner
ISBN 978-1-85792-627-9

Rocky Mountain Adventures by Betty Swinford
ISBN 978-1-85792-962-1

Scottish Highland Adventures by Catherine Mackenzie
ISBN 978-1-84550-281-2

Wild West Adventures by Donna Vann
ISBN 978-1-84550-065-8

THE JUNGLE DOCTOR SERIES

Jungle Doctor Meets a Lion by Paul White
ISBN: 978-1-84550-392-5

CHRISTIAN FOCUS PUBLICATIONS

Christian   Christian   CF4K   Mentor
Focus   Heritage

Christian Focus Publications publishes books for adults and children under its four main imprints: Christian Focus, CF4K, Mentor and Christian Heritage. Our books reflect our conviction that God's Word is reliable and Jesus is the way to know him, and live for ever with him.

Our children's publication list includes a Sunday School curriculum that covers pre-school to early teens, and puzzle and activity books. We also publish personal and family devotional titles, biographies and inspirational stories that children will love.

If you are looking for quality Bible teaching for children then we have an excellent range of Bible stories and age-specific theological books.

From pre-school board books to teenage apologetics, we have it covered!

Find us at our web page:
www.christianfocus.com

CF4•K
Because you're never
too young to know Jesus

'I remember hearing yells of "RAT!!" and then several piercing screams that would have put a girl to shame. I will admit I leapt up onto the bed near me, joining the three other guys already there! ...'

'Sometimes living in Asia can be hard. Especially when God tells my mum and dad what He wants them to do and I don't want to do it. So I asked God for something to prove to me we should move ...'

'Within seconds there were about 100 young people, some armed with iron bars. Our car was surrounded. Rocks were bouncing off the car like hail. The windscreen was hit a number of times and it was almost impossible to see out of ...'

'For the first time in my young life, I had to take the lead. It was a life or death situation. I was eight years old ...'

'When Jesus laid his hands on people they got better. Could we lay hands on our fridge and pray for it?' the kids asked Mum ...'

This book will give you a 'kids-eye' perspective of life in missions.

It has exciting, true stories, written by modern-day children whose parents are part of an international mission that is now 100 years old.

Some were present during major events in world history, some risked their lives on crocodile-infested rivers, others just needed a friend. The stories will reveal their hearts to you.

Edited by Jen Kallmier: Jen has long been fascinated by children's stories of God at work around the world. Perhaps she was inspired by her own three children, who grew up in Indonesia and Australia. With her husband Trevor, Jen has lived and worked in Indonesia, Australia, Singapore and England, their former roles of Regional Directors, then International Directors of they have visited families in many other countries.

WEC
reaching the unreached

CHRISTIAN FOCUS
PUBLICATIONS

www.christianfocus.com

ISBN 978-1-84550-981-1

9 781845 509811

Children's teaching and guidance, BIC - Children's teaching and guidance, BISAC - HRC/CHD/JBI, 8-12 yrs